PLASTIC'S REPUBLIC

ESSENTIAL POETS SERIES 260

ONTARIO ARTS COUNCIL
CONSEIL DES ARTS DE L'ONTARIO

an Ontario government agency
un organisme du gouvernement de l'Ontario

Canada Council   Conseil des arts
for the Arts   du Canada

Guernica Editions Inc. acknowledges the support
of the Canada Council for the Arts and the Ontario Arts Council.
The Ontario Arts Council is an agency of the Government of Ontario.
We acknowledge the financial support of the Government of Canada.

GIOVANNA RICCIO

PLASTIC'S
REPUBLIC

GUERNICA
EDITIONS
TORONTO • BUFFALO • LANCASTER (U.K.)
2019

Michael Mirolla, editor
Cover and interior design: Rafael Chimicatti
Cover image: Paolo Bona/Shutterstock.com
Guernica Editions Inc.
1569 Heritage Way, Oakville, (ON), Canada L6M 2Z7
2250 Military Road, Tonawanda, N.Y. 14150-6000 U.S.A.
www.guernicaeditions.com

Distributors:
University of Toronto Press Distribution,
5201 Dufferin Street, Toronto (ON), Canada M3H 5T8
Gazelle Book Services, White Cross Mills
High Town, Lancaster LA1 4XS U.K.

First edition.
Printed in Canada.

Legal Deposit – First Quarter
Library of Congress Catalog Card Number: 2018956516
Library and Archives Canada Cataloguing in Publication
Riccio, Giovanna, author
Plastic's Republic / Giovanna Riccio.

(Essential poets series ; 260)
Poems.
ISBN 978-1-77183-368-4 (softcover)

1. Barbie dolls--Poetry. I. Title. II. Series: Essential poets
series ; 260

PS8635.I23P53 2019   C811'.6   C2018-905167-1

For George Elliott Clarke

Virtuoso poet, gravitas-gilded scholar

Contents

AFTERLIFE (WORD)

FORE WORD
(PLAY)

The Gift

for Angelo

Lines of railroad tracks south of our
house, two misfit children mining
pop bottles, glint on glass sparking

gold two-penny promises. We piled small
change against the margin—a new home
we didn't recognize—until it claimed us.

Nickel and diming our dreams, we bought
dinky toys to zoom us to posh faraway streets,
foolish rings pressed cheap shadows on my fingers.

But the dolls I craved fancied well-heeled lives
in a world beyond our paltry stash—pricey girls
who stranded me on this side of the television.

By the time you landed a part-time job, I
ached for blush make-up and buff movie stars;
thwarted then your gift of a latecomer satin doll.

I never named her although we tried bonding
in reverse—the two of us locked in my room,
looking to backfill the past.

Homemade Wine

1

Boozy by eighteen, wine decants liberation, vino
rinses the skanky fallout of childhood's breach;
spirits flood wounds, soften petrified skin.

She's in the pink, swilling rosé at Rathskeller's,
downing fresh-faced luv fragmenting
in stem-glass valentines; snuggled in her boss's
blazing red Mustang, she's a tipsy, lipsticked rosebud
blushing over his wedding ring.

She's romanced wine since she was knee-high
to an oak barrel, kidding around in aromatic basements
making *mosto* with *papa*; musky pungence blends countries;
innocent reminiscence greens hunger's hills
where grape-flush trucks once pulled in.

Reared in Canadian autumns, playmate
to blonde wood crates loaded with California clusters
she's vined sweetness fermenting away—sport
for the house red's drinking games.

2

At twenty he's a lonesome immigrant marooned on
Saturday nights; gorgeous movies dishing
Marilyn Monroe and Jayne Mansfield;
each week, a Monday to Friday factory
of faux-flesh limbs, eerily plastic;
nine hours daily assembling girl-resembling dolls.
Blank-eyed babes end at five,

long evenings run on movie-stars,
he, broken-tongued, a de-starred silhouette
darkening. Solace comes from the *cantina*'s
gallon jugs of homemade; booze snuffs
the panic that he'll never feel at home again,
powers up flesh via a nine-year-old cousin,
jockeys Hollywood desires to a little thing …

3

She pours wine into each primal rite:
beginner's kiss, debut screw, first orgasm,
gulping red, white and rosé amnesia
to calm what's under her skin.
She imbibes young vin ordinaire, and
vintage Metaxa, Greek island plonk
buzzing in tumblers topped-up by soldiers on leave.
Cheap champagne spills over
her dancing Etruscan shoulders   she travels
with a body she minds
to states where no one knows her.

On Derek Walcott's island, the pop
of Dom Perignon uncorks true love,
under palms and volcanoes, a suitor tenders
aspirational flutes as prelude to French smooching; but

love goes flat when love's a face she can't
betray; best scatter to a one-night stand,
regroup in hangover's sunrise.

4

She would have liked, instead, to pour out words. Voice a head-
shake with phonemes for no. To point to a *bambola* just beyond
having; her passport to Canadian Girl. She would have liked to
string syllable after syllable, fit one word into the next and build
a body. Tell how limb by doll-limb (lifted from the factory), he
pieced his pleasure's hard swell and softening peak, her sticky
silence. First one doll leg, then the other. Next, the torso she
searched for that fault to find only a mound of shame. A left arm,
then the right. In expectation of the crowning blonde head: white
underwear, a striped satin dress cinched at the waist, shoes. But
... no head made good. Who can figure why? Will you believe her
when she says it ended at the neck; in a doll all dressed up with
no face to go?

5

She reads, drinks, dreams of love ... drinks
on some abandoned strand, drinks some more.

Till tongue and pen find ink, she'll miss
innocence (whatever that is).
On a moonstruck eve, all glitz,
again, she clinks champagne
(with whoever)
admires its pale gold, the foamy
head fizzing in inky air.

THE BARBIE SUITE

Plastic operates reciprocally to designate either a force that molds or a material that can be molded.

(Heather Warren-Crow)

Creation Myths

TURN I

A capital doll

Those who reproach injustice do so because they are afraid
not of doing it but of suffering it. So, Socrates, injustice,
if it is on a large enough scale, is stronger, freer and more masterly
than justice. And, as I said from the first, justice is what is advantageous
to the stronger, while injustice is to one's own profit and advantage.
(Republic, 344c)

A manic bon-vivant and eccentric spark, Jack Ryan hosted kooky, nightly parties—musts for A-list celebs, at his sprawling Beverley Hills haunt, "The Castle." Once a solitary, dyslexic whiz-kid, the unruly Yalie pulsed invention, pumped out patents before helming Mattel's Research and Design team and becoming the space-age collaborator with the company's founders, Ruth and Elliot Handler. Ruth—*the Mother of Barbie*—and her artist-husband courted Jack's brilliance and corporate know-how, made him a multi-millionaire with a royalty contract on all patents dreamt up by the head honcho of Mattel's best-and-brightest.

No pretty boy, Jack had a puffy, bird-like chest and helmet hairdo, elevated himself on Cuban heels and often swaggered a raccoon coat. Evenings entailed quirky fashions—costumes for the fantasy-life he staged at his mansion; his odd looks were overruled by a bankroll that earned him five foxy wives, including Zsa-Zsa Gabor.

Ruthless and open-handed, adored and despised, the man journalists nicknamed, *The Father of Barbie*, eventually crashed and burned, mind and body buried under an avalanche of court dox; *Mattel v. Ryan* tracks death by deposition, logs two hundred days of sworn questioning. *Mattel deposed Jack to death*, a co-worker quipped—corporate clout shamming Justice banished him from America's toy dynasty.

Weary of divvying up profits from Jack's ingenious fabrications, Ruth and Elliot fine-tuned their loot-grab as fair play, cleaving to technical obligations met, contractual promises honoured. Corporate deep pockets shifted Jack's rights to the Handler's left-hook as shrewd suits plied writs to steely ends—the courts blind to double-talking shills and diagrams reworked.

Chiseller-lawyers chipped away at his royalties: the legal score broke the bank. Jack's heart pounded at bygones as the good old days soured—bitterness thickened, rogue arteries clotted. Years of courtroom Latin paralyzed his larynx; his right side surrendered, then stiffened—the golden boy hammered to lead, his skull bloodshot. Obituaries in the *New York and LA Times* reported, death from "debilitation caused by a stroke." In reality, his one good hand fired a bullet into his bedridden genius; the ruddy mute lodged in his chest pooled on the floor where his wife, Magda, found him.

History is written by the victors. Ruth's version of Genesis was hatched from a Eureka moment brought on by catching her daughter Barbara's play with fantasy-stiffing paper dolls. Ever the virtuous mother, the Barbie name honoured her inspiration. For his part, Jack declared himself the mastermind behind their curvy concept and fashion flowering; he took the Lilli doll to Japan, negotiated materials, moulds and moolah and returned, Barbie prototype in hand. The appellation was a nod to his wife. After Jack's demise, Ruth's retelling grew noisier, killing any mention of her subordinate.

But Barbie's lineage is Teutonic; her forerunner is a sexist cartoon character whose seductions navigated a post-Hitler Germany. Ruth's blood quickened when she spotted the *Bild Lilli* doll in a Swiss store window. The plastic incarnation of the racy gold digger sold as a male novelty item is Barbie's smuggled European ancestor, the skeleton in Mattel's closet.

So, wise reader, bear in mind that, dollar-for-dollar, a collaborator and once-grateful patriarch can default to adversary and devour the lesser rank. Gold tips the scales so justice recalibrates as precedent; case law sets the argument: the gods hold court on Olympus.

On the Cusp

1936—the Nuremburg laws just a year old.
In Berlin, brown-shirted troops
scooped up riff-raff and race-mixers
as a guarded city came clean
for the Olympics: Lindbergh hobnobbing
with Hitler, Owens taking the gold.

I come from Warsaw Jews
but what did I care that in the old world
a Negro had jumped Dixie's white picket fence,
that a Jew could go to jail for screwing a German?

By Kristallnacht, we were in L.A.,
fat city of make-believe—me, a secretary
at Paramount, Elliot creating light fixtures,
a modern moon rising in his Plexiglas vision
for a new unbreakable country.

Into the first chapter of our American dream,
we needed samples for Elliot's décor designs—
let's buy our own equipment, I told him.
Setting up shop in our half of the rented garage,
I fuelled a hotter vision, my mind's eye
fired up the future—Elliot's quiet, artistic
unfolding, me jiving in sales and marketing.

I had no business know-how, just gumption
and bravado tempering doubt—clutching
the brass door knob warmed by my hand
I delivered myself, never again heard,
Get me a coffee, Doll.

My Barbie

My Barbie would one day fly solo, be
jet fuel for so many long shots,
but in the beginning, what was there?

Me. And the dolls of the United States
of America; hollow manufactured mothers
marooned in dollhouses, sham babies
in prams, the con of straight-bodied Ginnies
closing their weighted, sleeping eyes.

There was my daughter Barbara
dressing paper models, folding
her imagination over the country's
flattened women who weren't up
to navigating the future's curve.

Matt and Elliot were there—coupled
as *Mattel*; we had the Burp Gun
and Ukedoodle* and me, proposing this doll,
probing beyond male myopia.

Sure, Sputnik and Explorer were upon us,
in research and design, Jack was launching
toy rockets and engineering a hip angle
for my brainchild: he understood high energy
physics, how God is in the details, how
a beautiful girl has her own rate of spin.

* The Burp Gun and Ukedoodle were the first successful toys manufactured
  by Mattel.

Finding Lilli

We picked her up in Lucerne.

Barbara was 15, past toys by then—
Lilli was hard plastic, an elongated
doll with a shady past.

She was a piece of work:
her inverted heart hairline,
that single naïve lock silly-angled
across her gold digger's forehead,
her sidelong gaze framed
by eyebrows thin as a wispy thought,
the Japanese toymakers told us
she looked mean.

Her long legs fluted to black high-heeled
feet—almost too street. Yet the breasts
and waist were there, the rooted hair.

Imagination's fickle though—
it was the clothes Barbara loved.
I knew then, selling the outfits doll
by doll was all wrong, the play
is in dressing up, in knowing your own
floor-length dress and feather boa
can take you way past midnight.

Out of Step

Lilli doesn't travel alone
teetering on feet cast in unsettling
stilettos painted glossy black
she forfeits erect posture
for the ease of the odalisque position.

While Barbie broadens her horizons
Lilli will never step on Malibu Beach
mount a Harley or snag an Olympic medal.
After shopping New York, Barbie kicks off
her heels, though the arch remains.

Lilli's a male novelty, a leaner
doomed to kill time on dashboards
forced to forego the golf game, she
dangles from rear-view mirrors, reflecting
the future taking her from behind.

Always Barbie

Perfected
by Japanese finesse
I am mass production with breasts—
Barbara Millicent Roberts
a capital doll,
call me Barbie.
I am game
the axial daughter
of German pornography
and Lady Liberty's dream.

Polyvinyl enough
to co-opt every
trend, I keep
my always form
and face, change
career, colour, nation
and as positioning
requires twist
and turn
at the neck
and waist. Earning
my own cash
investing
in real estate
I travel
through time
and space

come boxed
complete
with a travelling case.

Among my favourite
accessories
is one named Ken.

So You're Barbie

An absent-minded theft,
the name-muddle—

were Barbie and Barbara both daughters?
Or maybe we were both her dolls,
this assumes equality though, and notice
how quickly words bleed ink without your consent.

I still put up with the paper doll
creation story, even retell myself how I
inspired that heady offspring, a chance collusion
feeding my mother's determination
to play God in the world of young girls.

Who names a busty play-girl with un-American
aspirations, after her own Yankee flesh and blood?
Was it an act of homage, of tender due
a public namesake when I needed
protection from too much modernity?

Most days, mom was all momentum
speeding off in her Thunderbird convertible,
drawn by the gravity of a miniature cosmos
the pull of tiny, manicured hands
the import of scaled waistbands and zippers.

Barbie, she'd sometimes call me
when it had always been Barbara
or Babs. Truth be told, didn't she
love Barbie more?

The Violence of Mirrors

The soothsayer,
sensing the violence of mirrors,
prophesied that Narcissus would only live
until the moment he saw himself.

Following that self-same impulse
for surface reflection, my mother
went missing, vanished
into big dreams made of small playthings.

I didn't want a designing dad
I wanted linoleum, turquoise
Formica spattered with black stars,
the mom business straight up.
When I complained, her love
bent back on itself, my deep longing
stilled in the face of her invention.

"I took care of the children or anything else,"
she informed the interviewer who asked
and blind to a double swap, we fell headfirst
into the afterlife made from our drowning.

Fathering My Barbie

That's me, Jack Ryan, a Yale buck made by Mattel royalties
an obsessive-compulsive dyslexic—IQ kinked to genius,
despite Ruth's maternal claim, I fathered Barbie.

That's me, with the Hawk and Sparrow III missiles, launching
Cold War toys for the Pentagon before hot-wheeling myself
into Jack Ryan, a young Yale buck beefed-up on Mattel royalties.

There's Ruth, all high school, a cocky, smart-ass skirt
a self-promoter loud as her pink, flip-top T-bird,
despite her maternal claim, I fathered Barbie.

Nursed on small love and small business, she's an all work
no play gal zooming to big bucks, scheming against me,
Jack Ryan, a young Yale buck high on Mattel royalties.

True, she lifted the sexy vixen, but I ferried Lilli to Japan,
nursed the mould past broken fingers and bubbled nose,
despite Ruth's maternal claim, I fathered Barbie.

I filed away nipples so Japanese toymakers knew American
values beat under the tight sweaters at Mattel—Barbie and Jack,
a Yale buck in my Bel-Air mansion erected on Mattel royalties.

Ruth highjacked the official story, starting with her daughter's
paper models, ending with me as a cut-out, backroom mechanic
me, Jack, Ryan, a stuck Yale buck stiffed of my Mattel royalties
despite Ruth's maternal claim, I fathered Barbie
                    (and every other huckster knockoff).

Plasticorations

*Images are pliable and can be sculpted like clay
and circulated like money.*
(Heather Warren-Crowe)

*Barbie remains the highest volume brand in the industry,
due in no small part to our ability to reintroduce the product
line year-after-year to fit the current life-styles of girls.*
(Mattel Annual Report, 1987)

TURN II

A more pose-able player

They're like us. Do you suppose, first of all, that these prisoners see anything of themselves and one another besides the shadows that the fire casts on the wall in front of them?
(Republic, 515b)

In a basement rec-room, a passel of pre-Barbie dolls dwell; chained to wood-panelled walls by the neck and legs, their pop-on heads fixed straight ahead on an outsized movie screen. Accessible via a pristine staircase rising to the sunlit ground floor, the front door leads outside. The inmates know no other reality for they have been peering at images cast on the screen since quitting the warehouse. Shackled to their tunnel vision, they remain oblivious to each other and the movie projector propped behind them emitting figures and objects made of nothing but celluloid, light and a recorded soundtrack. Year after year, the projectionist unspools dolly vignettes that convince the viewers that the life and lingo before them—this illusory shadow realm—is the one and only doll world.

The miniature human replicas consume toy company dramas grooming them for grown-up games that end in the good girl's good life. A shadow universe beams out pretty promise and though synthetic bodies feel cold and rigid, their docile glow warms to serious play.

Players-in-training bond with a *simpatica* female like Miss Revlon. She's genteel-chic with a jejune face and almost-there breasts—her wide-skirt and high heels fudging a blinkered ingénue who'll grow into the glassy-eyed Debbie Deluxe Bride made for virginal kisses. Layering on pearly lace, she runs a dress-rehearsal for the ritual June wedding. Her fragility, betrayed by imminent crackling is mended by Betty Bride flaunting a supple miracle vinyl, soft-selling a crack-proof helpmate who (de)flowers naturally to join the pram and diaper set. The missus swells from wife to mother via Tiny Tears weeping a watery drill; squeeze the belly and set baby bawling to rouse the necessary maternal instinct.

An unruly doll dawns in 1959 when one pre-Barbie goes rogue; squirming out of her chains, she swivels her neck away from the iron-fisted screen, spies the contraption spewing the light-borne, 2D world. Noting the slavish operator and celluloid feed, she questions everything. Turning towards the stairs, on the illuminated bottom step, she spots an animated woman clutching a foreign looking doll—a big-breasted coquette, all waist and legs, decked-out in a tight pencil skirt and décolletage. Beside the woman, a short dandy is talking up a trip to Japan, pushing a cutting-edge plastic. He's gaga over something called rotation moulding that can yield a detailed model and turn playtime into prophesy.

"I see," Barbie surmises, "there's no escaping this human world,"— and turning toward the Lilli doll—never looks back.

Eight incandescent years later, and Barbie is the zenith of a universal shift; the triumphal icon's ascent has Ideal Toys doing a 180 to get in on the fashion doll boom. But it's 1967 and she's looking old-hat despite bygone big-sellers like Bubblecut Barbie, channelling Jackie Kennedy, and the career highlight as an astronaut. It's an uphill climb to stay cutting-edge and the passé fifties-spawn is lacklustre; shades of Lilli haunt the look: kohl-lined eyes, averted gaze salon-slicked hair. Ur-Barbie surveys stale stiffs shadowing a derivative doll who quakes anytime mention is made of changing the mould.

Betty Friedan and Helen Gurley Brown have been cutting loose for years. It's "The Summer of Love" and Jack Ryan, the maverick last seen at the bottom of the stairs, longs to let his synthetic progeny swivel and boogie. Top doll deviates enough to spy him in his workshop, follows her inclination and pivots towards him. Propped on his lap, gazing deeply into his genius, she cajoles him to coax her vertical axis for the sexual revolution. Together they manoeuvre her hips this way, twist the upper torso that way, until she liberates in a counter-pose.

A panoramic view goes post-parochial, engenders a total about-face to a Mod Twist 'n' Turn Barbie. The knock-out crosses the Atlantic; on London's Carnaby Street, Mary Quant waits with a new, far-out wardrobe. Born-again Barbie grooves and gyrates out of the dim past into Mattel's hip, state-of-the-art Dream House.

Beyond Celebrity

In this manufactured world
a synthetic nature comes in handy.

A new doll every year
I reinvent myself in full view
of charging paparazzi
and crabby tabloids.

You'll find me
glamorous
famous
without the smashed-up fairy tale:
no drug-smeared stars
or bloated suicides
no last look back—no fade out.

I'm beyond that kind of matter,
don't need to redefine my terms
or explain my selves;
I'm posed for life and I
never bleed.

Proto Barbie (1959)

On essence

Shaped by post-war polymers and super molecules
by tough, egalitarian plastic, Barbie shares her can-do,
can-be-anything substance with pails and junk jewels.

Born a prototype, no original Barbie can be possessed,
her essence is reproduction, her being replication,
one face owned by millions indexes global success.

A resilient economist she feeds on public trend
relentless, shifty, peaking with each bend
she's a supply-side democrat—Barbie to the end.

On (re)production

Prone to inflation, Ruth spied a plane light dimming
on nifty-fifties paper dolls, conjured a becoming world
where a miniature woman clad in snazzy styles
dazzled the looking glass—here was an aspirational doll
whose detailed hands and Hollywood nails steered
a late-model car away from marriage and motherhood.

The male designers balked—said it couldn't
be done, until Ruth smuggled Lilli across the Atlantic
through tight-lipped Torch Girl's golden door.

But Lilli's rigid, injection-moulded body dictated
a new world re-vision—a fine-featured, soft-fleshed
citizen re-fashioned by industry's stylish chemistry.

This American promise craved a precision half method,
half matter, only a warmed-air slow burn
and a slow turn routed chipped fingers, a bubbled nose
only rotation moulding forged—from molten polyvinyl—
Barbie the hot newcomer.

And Hollywood make-up wizard Bud Westmore extracted
the bouncy teenager buried in Lilli's war-hardened face.
Curbing the trash, he unpuckered bee-stung lips
muted harlot-hard eyes, eased gaudy brows
until Barbie beamed up at him—her European
ancestor, mum in Mattel's closet.

On marketing

Via cleavage, non-stop legs and hair on overload
Barbie signals fashion's underhanded message,
at Mattel, brain-storming sessions—snarly male protests:

—no American mother will buy her daughter a doll with breasts.

Ruth headed for Madison Avenue,
procured branding patriarch, Ernest Dichter
whose Institute for Motivational Research
peddled theatre as psychodrama;
in *depth interviews*, Ernie scrutinized gesture,
probed prattle, distilled candour
into products fine-tuned to anxiety's balm—
all lack made good through consuming.

In sun-splashed playrooms
girls and mothers sized up:
Barbie as primordial American blonde
turned out in strapless evening frock
or chic summer suit—redhead Barbie

casual, in capris and car-coat
and brunette Barbie sparking
a sequin-gowned torch singer
or floating to bed in a frothy negligée.

The final analysis busted the girls' fancy
for curvy allure, but mothers pursed
Puritan lips at *the daddy doll with too much figure*

but the ad-man adept ferreted out the real deal
—*she's so well groomed*

So well-suited to a trailblazing TV ad turning
on a neat narrative—a teenaged all-American Barbie
who swims, dances, cheers on school teams
who's always spiffed up to run the show;
swanky and winning, she coaches a messy miss
          to pine for purses, gloves and more.

First pitched on the *Mickey Mouse Club,*
the new doll on the block crowns a spiral staircase,
a tiny, guiding foot steps into the everyday.

Twisting to the Times:
Twist 'n' Turn Barbie (1967)

Drafted by Jack Ryan and Steve Miller—
an engineering marvel and prodigy,
she taught those outmoded stiffs at Hasbro
a thing or two.

Barbie's discrete perpendicular bent turned on
Jack's prickly genius—how to overcome
such a mannered inclination?
                              Skew the vertical axis
away from the obvious, plot every miniscule pivot
tease each pin and joint until a swivelling hip eased
Barbie into a classic *contrapposto*, into a more
pose-able player who waved good-bye

to a Cold War past and played-out 50's face
made over to Mod with softly hued skin
rooted, *really for real* lashes
a long straight mane in your select colour:
sun-kissed blonde, red-head titian
chocolate bon-bon brunette.

But this fast-track Barbie, so keen to wow
and knock out all comers pitched
a Madison Avenue mercenary, her TV tender,
a hock-all turncoat:

Bring in your old Barbie for a half-price trade-in

Daughters swarmed dealers, lugging sold-out
forebears, scrapping the done-in cohort for a cool
quisling who—thirty days in—twisted
and turned in over a million American living rooms.

Eye Shift: Malibu Barbie (1971)

With a painted-on, averted gaze
irises shunted hard right, Barbie
artfully skirts the I, can't face
a gent eyeing her. Not agent
she evades the male scope
sidesteps the public offering
of fetishized body parts.

For a lifetime Barbie's sight
has glanced off billowing tear gas, steered
clear of Rosa Parks re-fusing the back
of the bus, of women setting bras ablaze,
draftees burning America's war card.

Like Manet's naked Olympia who pins
the viewer directly, the street pins
itself to Mattel's corporate window —
for the times, they are a'changin
and after Kent State—bullet holes
pepper Barbie's cellophane wall.

To turn a profit, this doll
can't afford vintage vision,
so a centred eye deploys a new-look
Barbie to the hip California scene
where she bypasses Berkeley

for Surfrider Beach. Recast as sun-kissed tender
her middling gaze directs cockeyed
liberation as Malibu Barbie surfs
the sales graph's peaking waves.

Totally Hair Barbie (1992)

This Barbie brushes archetypes as hair runs on,
extreme saran waves stream grazing
her feet; a girl can comb herself into a lavish
Lady Godiva or untangle Milton's wanton ringlets
to regain a Mattel-accessorized paradise.

Despite a gush of cool sheen,
this Barbie revives no restless grain-goddess
flowing into late-summer's cornucopia,
no Queen Berenice kisses curls good-bye
to forever pulse as love's star in myth's night sky.

This doll is hair-play as backlash babe—Fashion's
all-out war on short-haired flappers, pixie-cuts,
Sinead O'Connor's rockin' skinhead;
she's man's restoration of the Pre-Raphaelite femme.

And going brunette, she pitches a shoddy side;
nocturnes flow in waves crimping
a veiled witch loosening purse strings
and gotta-have-her storms. Cash swells—
store shelves ebb to bare as this totalizing
coiffeuse charms girls

into the outstretched arms of a beguiling Moloch.

The Ins and Outs of Earring Magic Ken (1993)

We're not in the habit of putting cock rings
into the hands of little girls.
  (Mattel Corporation)

On the brink of being dumped, a straight-laced Ken
launched a frontal assault on dowdy   anything
to hold his lady—Barbie's love keeps Ken.

Raving a deluge of hip, Ken bleached brown hair,
blew off the close-cropped military cut,
highlighted away reserve, exited the salon
a burnished, two-tone blonde—a textured kind of guy.

An all-smiles convert to the makeover, he piled on
vogue, let pecs steal through a lilac fish-net tank,
donned pink-stitched black jeans, a lavender leather vest,
trendy Italian loafers.   As Desire made good,

he flamed through stores out-finessing Earring Magic Barbie.

Ken might have survived sibylline pastels, the magic
earring ricocheting light, but the band dangling
from a neck-chain winked a cock ring, amended him to Gay Ken.

That flashy innuendo wedged Mattel between Middle America

and a hard place: business-as-usual recalled his present,
discontinued his future, erased Gay Ken back to the closet
and all free-thinking dolls mourned the toy-shelf's return
to the straight and narrow.

An insurgent stunner, this Ken sparked a munificent star,
pushed pink and blue to an all-embracing hue—cradled
in a buff, bold glow—Beauty's boyish, purple innocence.

Fulla (2003)

Born, blessed in Damascus, I
am a long-stemmed, lean
Middle Eastern Flower,
call me Fulla—a Barbie cover

minus bullet-bra breasts and bikini,
no arm piece boyfriend either,
I'm an appropriate doll, an in-the-pink suite
boxed with headscarf and blushing prayer rug.

But the doll revealed depends
on what must be concealed
I'm not always staged the same,
framed to flatter and revere, I veil
in line with national rule; my indoor
& outdoor outfits net high-class profit
from virtuous economics.

I'm a sable-eyed, olive-skinned,
kind of Barbie. TV ads jingle
my Muslim values—how a sexy
miss is happy to cook, read, pray,
to model prudent play when I
put on my virgin-spring abaya
and hijab before stepping out.

And male kin is no fashion bother
instead of Ken, a stylish older
brother corrects my look.

Mattel's Dark History (1967-2015)

When Black trends to beautiful,
Mattel integrates the toy shelf;
Black-like-me dye shades the Barbie visage,
Colored Francie soft-shoes into the doll 'hood.

Tinted to vacuum green from Black wallets,
Barbie's new friend looks swell, sells
by design but draws heat for the optical ruse
and off-colour name, for the supreme-Barbie
melanin patent below the brand.

1968 mandates a radical makeover:
yet Mattel makes do with Francie,
an *ethnically authentic* reduction
with planed nose, plush lips, abbreviated locks.

Talking Julie follows: archly exiting
her Diahann Carroll sit com on tawny heels;
the first real Black Barbie strings buyers past skin
to chatty alliance: "shopping is fun."

Black Barbie could have cracked the mould
but change argues high stakes—big bucks resist retooling

so pigment pours into subalterns
as the 70's waffle and Steffie hugs a Black twin,
the 80's go 'fro then lengthen in backlash,
then spiral up dazing Quick-Curl Cara,
and in the geography of Barbie collectables,
Nigerian and Jamaican reps colour nations
in costume, clip culture to folksy cliché.

The 90's melting pot quickens
when Shani, Asha, Nichelle and Jamal
proudly shuffle off the Soul Train flaunting
hip-hop pleather with Kente-cloth hints that reflect
the special style and beauty of the African-American people;
forever grinning, jointed arms and wrists
wave to success but locked knees ensure
dancers stay strictly inside the Mattel conga line.

In the 21st century, Ava Du Vernay,
director of *Selma,* dresses down—Art
offs Fashion in limited edition;
priced for adult collectors, she's one
of six Sheroes, hailed in a museum-meant
way—to be kept—not flexed in play

like the Obama Whitehouse spinoffs;
smart, So In Style Black dolls whose *distinct* skin
tones, angular cheekbones
back the same difference: their
lips full-er, hair curli-er, hips broad-er
than *Ur*-Barbie.

Trichelle Crosses Police Officer Barbie

As an Obama-White-House Black doll, Trichelle flaunts a fulsome head of ebony curls, outfits in African patterned leggings and a sleeveless shirt of blue forget-me-not blooms piped with gold. She's brains and beauty: Einstein I.Q., copper skin, her eyes, amber-flecked scouts—a visionary genius executing *Beauty* on canvas via pigment and brush. A graduate of New York City's Cooper Union, Trichelle's first show netted her a top-ranked art agent apt to tap U.S. tycoons looking to decorate a Palm Beach manse or Fifth Avenue apartment with dissonant art as cutting-edge stock. On such walls, novice works acquire the patina of posh; the critic's gaze bestows enviable savoir-faire to a prescient collector's eye.

Critics brand her a Frida Kahlo Basquiat blend—self-witnessing on oversized canvas—her emblematic Black body assailed and blitzed by state-sanctioned force, baring, for who can bear it, the inner and outer life of African-Americans balancing the pitching race tightrope. Buyers, it seems, hunger for craggy, abstract *Truth* and her next show sells out, bagging big money. A self-made woman, Trichelle moves to a roomy studio showcasing exposed brick walls; floor to ceiling windows cascade light on a big-time career, future luxe, charity events.

Long has Trichelle been hankering for a new vehicle; now that delivery and installation are no longer her purview, she can dump the rust-laced van. Plush with up-to-the-minute models, the Barbie-car showroom vaunts automobiles, campers, motor-bikes—all good for cruising with Skipper or Ken—but Trichelle, ever a seer, has free-wheelin' solo aspirations. Her blood races when she lays eyes on a sporty two-seater—the new 2012 Barbie Glam Convertible (doll included) draws involuntary caresses; she runs her hand over the pink lacquered body, lets it palm the Barbie silhouette hood-ornament. In her mind's eye, she sees herself as the driver to eventually replace that pale, rosy lightweight as *The Doll* starring in this package.

Cash slapped down, the Barbie's signature print interior must go; Trichelle designs a T-festooned pattern in regal purple to replace the B's and ditto with the letter change on the tire-rims. The customized coach arrives in June 2012; revving up for the maiden voyage, she's all smiles; America is righting itself, Obama en route to a second term despite Sarah Palin. Trichelle tours New York with unabashed pleasure. Her vehicle rocks. When pedestrians and fellow motorists check out the steering wheel, she's a declaration — a Black woman can, *yes, she can.*

But the Fates are just killing time until the snowy Christmas tide purls in, until Trichelle is purring home from an afternoon of gift-shopping when a cop-car pulls into her rear-view mirror then glides into the lane beside her. Its siren momentarily censors the carols, and she is pulled over. Blonde, pony-tailed, Officer Barbie (badge # 53) tags the license plate and although the record is spotless, she exits her cruiser, opens her hand for the driver's license and ownership documents. Trichelle obliges but not without asking why she is being stopped. Officer Barbie informs her that the left, front headlight is out. The incredulous driver leans out to look, the policewoman taps the light's glass cover, bares her teeth and declares that, somehow, the light is now working: "Must be a short."

Officer Barbie figures that a search will produce illegal drugs; surely this well-heeled *Negro* woman could not afford this car unless she is dealing (or is a mule — being a woman and all). Anxiety squeezes Trichelle's throat as she is ordered out of her safe zone, she knows NYC's finest are no protection for her. The uniform shoves the artist up against the cruiser and runs tyrannical mitts over Trichelle's tense figure. Each paw patting down her body is a muted slap, each handprint etching her skin requires a retreat to mind, a calming interior monologue to squelch the desire to accuse and cuff, to provide a pretext for a beating or worse still, a shooting — and all in the name of The Law.

Officer Barbie orders the now-shaken driver to stand manne-quin-still and transfers her attention to the car where she rips fine wrapping paper off boxes and tips contents out of gift bags. Finally, flashlight beams bear down as she lasers the trunk and all nooks and crannies to come up empty-handed. Disappointment colours officious Barbie's tone as she tells Trichelle she's free to go. "Get that headlight fixed," she yells before evaporating into traffic.

Surmising that gender is no shield from police violence, Trichelle takes this lesson straight to Art. In her sun-infused studio, she assembles pots of pigment, an array of palette knives, brushes of sable, camel-hair and hog bristle. On blank, gesso-washed can-vasses she begins lashing out crimson strokes that jag colour and line into chaotic faces whose oversized eyes spiral into the endless news of assaulted Blacks—an American community assailed, bru-talized, injured, sometimes shot in the back or at point-blank range on impulse and no recourse to justice.

Chronicled in newspapers and on ubiquitous screens, muscled into memory, the rattle of random wrongs, gratuitous force and impro-vised judgment shape her vision. A fury of limbs bolt flesh onto steely weaponry; bodies sunder and reform, rattling summer streets and oxblood-scored apartment blocks. Under siege, the Black body drags a ball and chain in the tempered steel of prison statistics; impasto thickens paint with pulpy clout until force loses boundaries—frac-tures a spine, collapses lungs. Trichelle scars and mutilates surfaces, executes skinless faces as cross-sections of mental interiors: murder's shell-shock, terror's essential vigilance, widowed and orphaned rooms—anger's communal voice bereft in tonal concrete. The show, titled *Body Cop: Body Shop*, launches on Valentine's Day 2014.

On May 3rd 2014, around 1 a.m., Trichelle is powering home from late night festivities after a panel discussion on the exhibit. Over-tired and miffed by an especially virulent attack by a pasty-faced art critic, she momentarily drifts and loses control; the car feels willful and unresponsive. At the corner of Polar and Queen, the front glam-wheels slam into a pole. The windshield crackles into butterfly wings and her ensuing behaviour suggests that she may have struck her head. A resident, awakened by the collision calls 911 alerting the Barbie Police Department that an accident may have occurred and a woman was wandering the street looking "discombobulated," maybe "dangerous."

At 2:14 a.m. Officer Barbie sporting a brunette ponytail (badge #77) and her partner Officer Ken, blaze though the streets, siren searing the air, the cruiser's rooftop flasher splashing blood on the night sky. To avoid alarming the citizenry, they kill the squad car's wail on approaching the neighbourhood. The two officers exit on hyper-alert. Adrenalin-juiced by the eerily silent street, Officer Barbie draws her gun, keeps it at the ready, body-close. In her notes, she describes how she proceeded down a lamp lit Polar Avenue, how, in the distance, she spotted a figure *charging* towards her. "Stop right there!" she remembers calling out. But Trichelle kept coming, bee-lining toward the officer, probably assuming help was in sight. In her right hand, she waved a bright metallic object that turned out—later—to be her younger sister's majorette baton.

Reflex-fear bruises the scene and propels a seasoned policewoman into a reptilian-brain blind reflex where a Black face signs danger, even death; flashing metal can only signal a weapon. Officer Barbie raises her Glock 17 and discharges six bullets into the artist's body. Trichelle crumples to the ground; Melpomene* starts out of sleep, wakes from another violent nightmare where rain pours on row upon row of blank canvasses.

* In Greek mythology, one of the nine muses; the muse of Tragedy.

Imperial Barbie: Dolls of the World (1964-)

Fit for expansionist strategies, ready to Uncle Sam serve
Mattel induces fine-figured folk, tots up a planet filled
With *Barbie Dolls of the World* styled to manifest destiny's verve.

Powered by that pulsing beacon atop a *city on the hill*
Ethnic sired charmers fashion exotic conspirators
And in each colonized face, Yankee beauty is instilled.

Kimono-clad and obi-bound, Barbie invades Japan in '64,
Then donning her annexed grass skirt, she aces
Choice South Pacific Islands—seizes public assets galore.

Game to couture culture, glamour's secular body displaces
The eagle's looming wings, preferring dainty manicured hands.
In Korea, Spain, the Arctic, Barbie settles her Janus-faces,

Dolls up civics, lends her name to hyphen all motherlands.
Adopting typical portraits girls globe trot and assert
Mannered, kid-around scripts a smug poseur pens.

The first Amerindian Barbie christened "Spirit of the Earth"
Spawned six more gals garbed in buckskin discourse,
Oodles of fringe and feathers, milk for all she's worth

Princess Pocahontas rising beatific on beaded toes,
And when critics cry foul, Design brings on fabrication
Of a pair of chilling Barbies—eponymous *Eskimos,*

Mattel retorts: *traditional garb and feathers, stress our veneration*
Of indigenous culture; these keepsakes suit a popular fancy
For native clothing and artifacts—we intend no appropriation,

Though one elder decrees, "Despite fake threads, Barbie I can see."
Now any polymer empire calls for noble daughters—
Select, self-crowned blue-bloods, fit for romancing

A nouveau-riche republic keen on old-world hauteur
Recycling a Barbie visage that crafts a token attired
In muddled regalia spouting polity as folkloric natter.

As the plumed princess from Mexico is Aztec inspired
So, the Cleopatra Barbie is highborn from the Nile
But South Africa's arched, royal feet must get very tired

From tip toeing shoeless, in *traditional Ndebele* guile.
No matter if oblivious aristocrats trample national regard
With aloha allusions—history as bling and style,

These fad-wise sovereigns rule as trophy eBay stars.
But Barbie cannot doze on the laurels of her success
A free market exacts demands on shareholders' avatars.

Across Einstein's universe, may rococo ventures God bless
Like the *Landmark Collection* built on taffeta's structural mirth
Transforming stately icons to gowns parading burlesque:

Big Ben peals from B's belly, The Eiffel Tower fans to a skirt,
While Sydney's opera house pleats on chiffon shoulders,
And Liberty high hands two dresses, fitting exceptional worth.

Let the first month's lunar light gild glamour's soldier,
Our New Year China doll ringing-in the *World
Festivals Collection*—in thigh-slit silk, behold her

Winking at reserve; a Mandarin-collared girl
Decked out as red fertility plying lucky money.
Now gear up Diwali and Brazilian dancers swirling

Into costume parties, a crush of spirits sunning
gloom with lamps or a yearly pre-Lenten ball.
Gear-up Mexico's recall, in peasant chic punning

Cinco de Mayo's freedom-fighters who all
Bravely trounced the French Imperial army,
Or folks widening Main Street—*Dreamers* so-called.

When the Berlin Wall collapsed, Mattel's emissary warmly
Reached out to welcome *Freundschafts* Barbie to the market,
Boxing Freedom's twins, Communism's bad karma;

The E.U. doll friends left, to the right America works it,
pom-poms cheering on a bossy watch-me manner
Refined from decades of pushing a western racket.

When lack of a social conscience prompts, "time to can her,"
The '90 Barbie Summit dares a kick-ass kiddy-caucus;
Innocents from 28 countries, under Mattel's banner

Consider worldly concerns while shielded from raucous
Jobbery in far-off sweatshops—Barbie's invisible body
Scarfed by first-world shysters. Ingénues opt instead to focus

Sweetly on peace and planet; dovely ads proudly
Trumpet Summit Barbie's social-justice import
By donating part of her sales while Mattel sells bloody

Largesse under *Marketing* in the Annual Report.
Borne aloft on naïve hands, a stately Liberty supreme,
Rehabilitated, Barbie rises, a blonde lamé retort.

What's old is new again—year's end gowns the esteemed
Fancy-ball holiday models, three hued in complexion,
Triple too-bright belles—Mattel's top-doll regime

Tolls a thumbs-up Barbie, strutting resurrection.

A Happy Fiftieth (2009)

I've outlived Betsy Wetsy
and Chatty Cathy, bypassed
diapers, bibbed dresses, cute baby janes.
I'm not arrested mothering
and never a finished woman,
since Malibu, 1971, my once-sideways gaze,
looks straight into Everygirl's heart.

I'm plastic
in the original sense of the word,
the matter behind your need
for personal theatre, for the preview.
Calculated to be pivotal
I'm a living doll selling
my own bill of goods.

Many have traced me
but none racked up my success.

I'm a 50-year-old publicly traded doll,
always Barbie
playing to a made-up moment
in a reality near you.

Identity Crisis (2016)

1

Mattel's Design head honcho plots it *de novo*:
first to plunge, all-out, into the fashion-doll fray,
cheeky glamour going toe-to-delicate-toe
with goody-two-shoes and play-it-safe poupées,
Barbie's bolt to the top demanded
that singular, hard-nosed shell—an on-target
doll-house for trained story, pointed reverie.

Our model cat-walked stores—blonde,
blue-eyed booty rustling restless pockets.
Right from the get-go, virago pluck
yielded global play so 1 Barbie zipped past
a cash register every 2 seconds—the brand
unrolling 1 billion per annum, unrivalled
thru 150 countries; Mattel's universe a'swell,

year in, year out until Barbie slumped,
dissed by post-modern moms slamming
conscious wallets shut.

Ever a feminist—the pioneer's defense—
Barbie always ranked money-in-the-bank,
flaunted freewheeling cars and homes,
and early on, umpteen careers counter frontal attacks:
business woman in '63, astronaut in '65

but on NASA's earthy base, anatomy eclipses space gear.

A resounding knell as Disney's princess moves
out of Mattel's castle, as *Lego Friends* muscle in
and *Elsa* freezes Barbie's high-roller score;
the battered warrior blushes—
nose-diving numbers demand dutiful shame.

2

Profit's diktat fires naysayers—five decades
of game-changing grit needs sifting!
Barbie-hater surveys & focus groups fork over
the skinny; losses spawn Project Dawn
to reform the single figure fascista,
appending three *body-types* optioned from
Barbie's plastic matrix.

In marketing, lexical headaches, semantic brawls:
"tall, petite, curvy & original (?Barbie)"

All risky lingo, for who can forecast gist?
Who can speculate when *curvy Barbie*
will gift to *fat* and backfire? Someone's
bound to raise Cain, so chance a few pounds,
a benign modifier and Barbie rings in 2016,
as a belly and butt silhouette flat-footing
the cover of *Time*.

15 fresh Kens enlist, fortify the Fashionista
New Crew of 43 trendsetters—diversity
as second skin: black, brown, tawny, fair
& freckled diplomats beg forgiveness for past wrongs,
countenance 14 new faces as cheekbones morph,
noses broaden or narrow, eyes slant and widen;
comb in the long and short of politic hair,
make blue-eyed amends with 18 new iris hues.

Spawn the nod, overwhelm demand.

But a fluid Barbie baffles Mattel's existential stamp,
as the mould breaks down, the brand bleeds
and Dr. Barbie's psychiatry office is standing room only.
Fashionistas of all stripes, in sneakers and stilettos,
tiptoe on eggshells, testing each other—*Are you Barbie?*

Do I look like Barbie to you?

Callow Inspiration: Frida Kahlo Barbie (2018)

Because a girl cannot be what she cannot see.
(Mattel Corporation)

Scarred by polio's primer, she painted
a death-masked toddler gripping a lone flower,
Death recharged, derailed a trolley,
fractured her spinal column; a high-spirited
teenager bound in a gesso-white body-cast,
she munched on pale sugar skulls,
confronted her accidental escort.

Reflection and ennui provoked fierce Muse
as blank canvas, loneliness as newfound agent;
the sick-bed transformed to atelier
and Frida Kahlo—painter, model and portrait
fleshing out the void with form and colour.

Once off her back, she kept company
with a commie-femme photographer,
Chileno bard and anti-Stalin Bolshevik,
wed a bon vivant mural artist whose wine of choice
had to be full-bodied, banner-red,
the gold of his labour sweetening
Mexico's walls and plutocrat plazas,
foregrounding erased miners and sugar-cane workers.

But Frida's brush decanted art from slant anatomy,
limned a spinal itinerary nailed to a steel corset,
rendered her body as biological epic: its sickbay odyssey,
marital lacerations, cinematic paramours—
a womanly dialectic of love and loss.

Her dress composed a *mestizio* manifesto:
chartreuse parrots and solar dahlias
aflutter in billowing, lace-fringed skirts
and embroidered blouses; obsidian hair piled
to a native headdress crowned with ribbon,
butterfly wings or floral nests stressed
that neither Paris nor New York could occupy
her closet or colonize her easel.

Frida's signature unibrow
and ghost-moustache insisted facial hair
is no strike against Beauty unless she be prisoner
to Don Juan's gaze.

Imagine then, International Women's Day—
the debut of gravitas-primped Barbie pimping
Frida (Barbie) Kahlo as "iconic inspirational woman,"
more brow-beaten than unibrowed,
her bald upper lip, reedy neck and stick-figure arms
gringo the role-model as a rip off artist
playing to the mommy sweet spot;
a vacant-faced, feint-Frida to thin out
the competition and expand the brand
to its rightful take of the feminist pie.

Barbie never admits her falsie-logic
and dark-plastic art, cannot unpluck
or as youthful radical, brandish
the hammer and sickle;

a hollow tribute—Barbie can only see,
the callow Frida she opts to be.

Human Barbies

We have no intention of growing old
as defined by previous generations.
(Cindy Jackson)

I was born in the wrong body and I have spent
my entire life trying to reveal the real me.
(Rodrigo Alves)

TURN III

Not imitating nature but replacing her

*What about someone who believes in beautiful things, but doesn't believe
in the beautiful itself and isn't able to follow anyone who could lead him to the
knowledge of it? Don't you think he is living in a dream rather than a wakened
state? Isn't this dreaming: whether asleep or awake, to think that a likeness
is not a likeness but rather the thing itself that it is like?*

(Republic, 476c)

Had Narcissus lived to recount his fatal descent to Hades through
his selfsame idol, he would caution against drowning in your own
eyes. A mirror depends on the optics of light and being to diffuse
a second-hand sun, and in its lambent radiance a child catches the
glimmer of a shady figure. Innocents learn to heed its silver-plated
draw, to trust the magnetizing double. Cindy grew up walled in by
a persistent mirror, colliding with a reflected malcontent shackled
to her by the image-making human lens. To hear her tell it, she first
met Barbie at the age of six and instantly fell in love with the min-
iature ideal that fostered a *living doll*. The first mortal participant in
the Barbie form, Cindy would be reborn as a forever-unfinished girl.

* * *

A winged half-naked Rodrigo decked out as a white angel, once kissed
Justin for the camera. In the green room at a conference for Plastic Pos-
itive adepts and aficionados, the two tabloid and YouTube celebs meet
up again. Eyeing himself in the mirror, Justin, who calls himself The
Original Human Ken, is aghast; he should be wearing his "Proud to
be Plastic" muscle shirt but looks like Southern Gentleman Ken in a
white linen suit with matching footwear. Rodrigo floats towards him,
a peppy cherub in a pearly tutu and snow-owl wings, a moon-lit halo
atop his bleached hair (transplant).

All-mirror walls envelop the room in infinite reflections: it's image upon image of Justin and Rodrigo as far as the eye can see. But a pink princess froths the ivory waves when Cindy sails in—gowned, crowned—grooving a Disney vibe. Hugs all around as the two plastic-positive reps gush admiration for the esteemed, original Human Barbie.

They're all supposed to be conference presenters, but something's gone awry. "Where are we? Is this a dream?" Rodrigo's innate mischief surfaces as he flaps his arms and skips around the room.

"Whoa!" Justin squeals. "This is too weird: it's like we're prisoners in a hall of mirrors or like we've been dumped down a rabbit hole into a universe populated only by—us—crazy!"

Cindy is at a loss for words; she should be all diva-vixen in Dolce and Gabbana, eliciting secret glances of admiration or curiosity. She's no synthetic extremist like these two nut-bars who know nothing about Da Vinci and the sublime—her Renaissance ideal.

"Proud to be plastic," Rodrigo shouts out. "We're in heaven, Cindy."

But Cindy is transfixed by the oversized wall monitor screening a video. She freezes as subtitles reveal someone is under the knife. "Rodrigo, is that you on the screen undergoing a procedure?" Cringing at the scarlet on the surgeon's gloves, she turns away, examines the subject's unnerving face: pronounced cat eyes, cantilevered cheekbones and taut, luminescent skin render a frozen, impenetrable mask—so out there.

"Yup," Rodrigo nods, "I live-streamed having four ribs removed to narrow my waist. If you keep watching you'll see them. The surgeon wanted me to bank those babies, but I took them home in the end. Still got 'em in a jar."

She can't bear the close up of bloody bone against the creamy cotton towel. Her book, *Living Doll*, bios her metamorphosis as "the organic evolution" of an ageless socialite. These jokers twisting plastic into internet performance art belong to another world.

"Hmmm ... the recovery must have hurt more than usual."

"Not so bad. It took five inches off my waist; problem is, I don't feel any smaller, though my corset helps a bit. It's so unreal how hard it is to stay slim after thirty; a twenty-inch waist is my wish. Beauty's all unnatural—that's why they call it make-up and dressing up. After fighting my genes, I turned plastic positive to follow my creative fluidity. I'm my own work of art—always in progress."

Countless reflections of the trio beckon from the walls, but they're drawn to a new face on screen. "OMG!" Justin screams. "That's me. Hey, I know which video that is; I live-streamed my back implants to showcase my beauty-broker start-up and to introduce myself as a custom implant designer. You'll see my drawings and diagrams. I'm the first person to have a latissimus implant on my back. I love the ability to design and brand my body."

"Wow, Justin, that's so cool! You should be wearing a muscle shirt." Rodrigo adjusts his tipping halo.

"I *was* wearing one, before I landed here. People call me a narcissist and some so-called experts say that I suffer from body dysmorphic disorder because of my three-hundred-plus procedures. But I am really a born creator. Pioneers have always been called loony and been pooh-poohed; look at Picasso or Monet. Why do people get so stuck on the natural human form? I don't see why I shouldn't have total control like any artist has over his work."

Cindy smiles animating the tug of ancestral dimples on her suave, sixty-something face.

"I think of myself as an artist too, but prefer classical beauty."

Another turnover in the YouTube drama and there she is, a sixty-something, busty pinup and femme-fatale defying Mother Nature, "Look at me and Valeria together on Russia's biggest talk show." All enthusiasm now she takes up Valeria's cause, "You must know her; people stupidly call her Ukrainian Barbie, but she's not plastic, she's real—not just smoke and mirrors or Photoshop—so gorgeous, so ethereal."

"I'm not sure about her," Justin says shifting his attention to the looking glass—maybe he needs to have that forehead vein sliced and flattened.

In this self-perpetuating wonderland, the three captives wait to be escorted to the stage. Silently sipping Evian water, they roll into the reflections of their bodies and faces; above them float frames of skin sliced and parted, of blood flowing into silicone.

Plastic's Republic

On the cusp of the age of "Better Living through Chemistry," carbon atoms dance along a molecular backbone. In his lab, bright with industry-incandescent vision, the chemist, hankering for a sci-fi lab coat, follows fibre and air filaments, chains particles until miracle yarns form, until Nylon, Orlon, and Crimplene bless us with a wrinkle-free world.

In neon cities and fireplace towns of America, copycat synthetics flourish. Old world gold, emeralds, silk and crystal morph to a citizen's republic of faux opulence. Being meshes with seeming—natural law bewildered by a chaos of replicas. Everywhere, anodyne displays populated by old-school dolls get a wake-up call from Barbie, a chic stars-and-stripes teen who toys with Beauty and confounds Truth. Restive as a budding champ, she embraces time by outwitting its horizon, tops the competition by outprettying them through synthetic selection. No face, no body, no narrative checks her expansion. Forever becoming, she gets this pliable stuff, prophesies that the land will resin-ate with ductile desire and yielding identities. She is Darwin's dream-femme.

"On this I will mould my empire," Barbie declares and ditches the cardboard Dream House for a plastic A-frame. In her new digs, the décor celebrates plastic's conquest. After hanging the Warhol and Barbie-and-Ken portrait on pink latex walls, she sits on an acrylic slipper chair, loosens her ponytail, lets down her hair, and admires Lucite vases fluting wilt-proof roses. She's peachy-keen on the garden walled by mock-stone, on all-season grass and vivid flower beds impervious to drought and deluge.

Bestowing topnotch benevolence, Barbie adopts Cindy Jackson, an adoring six-year-old fan. Hand in hand, they tour the new three-storey house, stroll past the cerise baby grand and spiral staircase until they reach the huge bathroom flaunting a floor-to-ceiling portrait of the proprietor. Seated before posh vanities, they swivel play-fully. In a light-studded mirror, Barbie locks eyes with this young Barbie-to-be. "We are not imitating nature but replacing her," she declares. "You will overcome the barb of human birth. An uncanny escape artist, you will embody opposing truths; others will covet your conquest and aspire to be—at last—self-determined Beauty."

Human Barbie—Matter Over Mind

1

The first time Barbie came for the freckled babe
I want to look like that, sounded
in Cindy's six-year-old psyche—even so,
she might have let her Mensa-to-be

argue for an everyday belle, squelched
the ersatz siren-call to deem face and body as poor kin
needing a makeover before being loved.

Rather than allowing Barbie to arrest her look,
she might have played it out, held the pretty puppet
to transitional fetish—outgrown the doll phase.

Instead, she grew up plotting the dimpled farm girl's rout
continued to runway-rank mouth, cheeks, chin
to dream of other Cindy forms via mirror skins.

At thirty-three, Barbie called again; as the family bequest
smoked her palms, Cindy spurned genetic flesh,
kicked off her carnal devotion to an arch-footed totem.

2

First hike the eyes, trim a jut of chin
implant high cheeks, desquamate your skin

now syringe derma-filler, shuttle fat
reshape a slack jaw, elevate the butt

rhinoplast a first schnoz for one preferred
upgrade the second for a button-nose third

and on, for years Cindy dolls up—refleshes
being Beauty's chameleon eternally refreshes

be a shapeshifter's archive, a Human Barbie hit
hook women craving change, those resisting it

morph as Art's madonna, a plastic surgery sage
a *Guinness Book* record holder, an age-

less Aquarian, a truly self-made creature
the dimples I was born with remain my sole original feature.

Cindy Retorts

Christen me a skin-deep fake,
a scalpel-sculpted doll
confer snide, inhuman(e) epithets:
Bionic Woman, Human Barbie,

Cut me off from you—
a lunar lady, submissive to natural
history, biding gravity's drag;
but the tarnished Golden Rule you bare

fudges Beauty's primary place,
I'm social capital, the meat and muscle
of female looks as money in the bank
and since we all rank the stock

meet my perfect face, let spite
trace a crafty, constant woman
unclocking the fountain of youth;
consider me as anti-memoir, a truth

test, the time-line's correlation
between looks and success—I am
overcoming, I—made over a plain girl
and over my too ordinary art

and over routine rejection,
now, my part? American youth culture
sutured to Leonardo symmetry,
I'm a perpetual rite of passage, forever

turning heads, my de-flawed face,
nip 'n' tucked shape unlock a high
society claiming synthetic nirvana
as its club price; from weathered shadows

I select and shade the fittest Cindy
to swim in life's shallows, the deep
no longer warrants such sad vigil and decline—
these *your* rooms I work,

this *your* air I buy; Beauty is power,
low-status looks avenged, a wisdom body,
iconic and iconoclast;
power's beauty is my best revenge.

Plastic-Positive: Rodrigo Alves
The Human Ken

A heartbreak it was coming of age
the worst kind of youth,
the body bullied and you,
such a tender boy, an innocent shut
in flesh and all its cagey bars.

Insoluble words: the belly-pouf
love-handles, man-boobs;

chin too square, the Negroid nose shoved
into a urinal and you, a blubbering dummy
ripe for dysmorphia's mindful master
to pull on the night-light, switch reflection.

A tragedy coming of age on television
in the surgical contours of the rich and famous,
ever on mirror watch fielding flabby,
ego-needling wrongs. To arrive banished each day
on the other side of that physique—quixotic
a loser exacting a life's work to extract error—
reap a bona fide self.

Bequeathing elders soon bankroll
that birthright—your eyes Buñuel lancets
floating on screens where the con-art carving
of Hollywood hacks render cutting-edge muses
from synthetic stone.

You the nose job, cheek implant, justified jaw
you chiselled and chastised,
you mirror   not-you;

self-sighted creator, piqued cheek bones,
pec implants, peek-a-boo cat-eyes
not-again   you;

no sweat, the fake six pack—YouTube gore
streaming live—press on
to the man inherent in plastic;

to dissect sans atlas, piece together the opus
then unpiecing four ribs, be both Adam and Eve.

A few days on you're a post-op, photo-op
checked-out in the tabloids doin' the harlequin strut,
tube draining toxins, stylish the flow
colour-tied to your jacket, blood-satin-lined;
flash the martyr's cup pooling crimson—a thorny
eyed Son's own sacred heart

for Beauty crucifies,
an overweight mind layers on fat;
your seeker's waist, looking no thinner
you feel no smaller lost in God's gaze;

alone in the dark—stabbing lungs, damned breathing—
where's the incision to flat line the screen?

But diffuse, in the glow, your flock's bearing witness,
post after post, just one more passion play
remember transcendence   one choice cut away.

Valeria Lukyanova: Breatharian Barbie
(a.k.a. Ukrainian Barbie)

To astrally project, subsist on air,
operate online and ply a cyber blade;
to quit the body pound by inch
and with a brush of ether tuft chart
a ciphered self

To bolt from earth as light
be noumenal silver soaring above
the shuddering world-wide web

a reborn star-child, outshining human ends.

Justin Jedlica Slams Ukrainian Barbie

1

A miming manga is Valeria,
a dead mannequin,
daring to size up this *real* Human Barbie,
I cast a diva all implant 'n' glitz,
best off, as a leading lady for me
the original Human Ken;
but my kiss-kiss, cheek-cheek
brushed a still life—glanced-off
this Photoshop master's 2-D façade,
she's just another anorexic vamping
for Twitter applause.

2

Inside Edition—stage for fanfare news—
got word that *East Bloc Barbie*
was touring the U.S. of A
one more Hollywood wannabe—sure
but handy for upping my buzz.

Digging into her background
I unearthed GQ's tell-all,
and after our mash-up, wondered
what if this once-teenage Goth
had stayed a night-vision prowler
slumming Odessa's down side?
Might her spiked leather cuffs
have signalled a punk-rock pussycat
clawing at Putin's spotlight?

Through a wall of pics, I trace Valeria
forming on screen—how she steals
through the image wielding *the liquefy tool,*
lacing virtual cuts that off flesh and bone,
cinching her cyber-corset;
then fusing white lie
with pale light, she deftly emerges—
an imago, impossibly Nordic.

Zero-eyed, her kohl-tattooed anime stare
when she uplifts a boa for Instagram gawkers,
viral snake charmer and serpent sloughing
digital skin, she curates each Barbie-macabre
onto the scene.

3

Since showbiz turns on
a zealot's physique, this New Age saint
loves *prodigious fasting;* inhales low-cal
smoothies, feasts on sun and air,
dead-sure spirit feeds wafer-thin flesh.

Yet this pixel riddle serves no God,
preaching instead, her own timeless Truth,
a make-up ace and branding trompe l'oeil,
she bolts from flesh to mystic Amatue*
guiding astral seekers and acolytes
via YouTube's subtle body delights.

4

This is no plastic surgery champ,
only a Photoshop babe spouting a cold-blooded
mean, claiming Beauty's sin is reckless
race-mixing; thankful Art restores
the Aryan norm.

For our real-time on camera—
no chat, no kidding, no give-and-take flow.
Why all the drumrolls? No live TV here,
only a lifeless drag queen caught in the spotlight.

* Amatue is Valeria Lukyanova's chosen spiritual name and brand;
her alter-ego provider of lectures and self-help videos.

Valeria Upbraids Justin

Dear Justin,

Since English curdles on my Ukrainian tongue,
I came across as mute, but here
write stylishly having hired a starving
poet to drift, ghostly, through my clumsy
prose, sift out verbal blunders, make up
and dress up this payback for your smug
YouTube slam after my flowery Barbie
and your wooden Ken "duet"
on *First Edition.*

If you're not too busy ogling that dodgy
snob reflected in your looking glass or
screen, note that I wrote Ukrainian—
not Russian. Having scanned a few interviews,
scrutinized an article or two—clearly
you fancy yourself as more than a boy-toy,
tell how you bypassed sports and fancy cars,
fed your true passion by sketching and chiselling
the human form—venerating the classic
symmetry glorified by Greece
via a suspect Adonis resonant (for you)
in that tiny Mattel man.

But do google *The Soviet Bloc*
and discover its blocks leaned west,
then toppled along with the Berlin Wall in '89.
So, blowing me off as *Eastern Bloc Barbie*
and Russian is Ugly American Ken
showing GI Joe ignorance. Please tell
me that, on occasion, propped in this
or that position, on the mend from pec

or butt implants, you gingerly grab
a slice of CNN—perhaps you've heard
of Crimea—no? I could get touchy
about such airhead slips, if you get my drift.

You need to muzzle your Juvaderm-juiced
lips, quit spitting nonsense about being
a "true body mod" nattering on, that
I'm a fake Human Barbie, unfit to share
your candid camera since I'm no
surgery soap-opera—not plastic-
permanent, as you put it.

What does *true* mean when applied
to a pampered boy whose claim
to fame is hundreds of drastic doctorings?
Maybe "true body" and Justin Jedlica
should not score the same sentence.

Did I read you right—that you are more
real than me? That your deadpan face
is morally superior because it doesn't wash
off at night, and your invasive pecs
and abs are not (like me) "just for the digital?"
You want me to believe all the nips,
and needles—the fillers and tucks
are for your eyes only? (And I wonder
castrato, what else you've had cropped)—Oh,
to look in the mirror as lover and beloved
and say, behold such fine art, my own magnum opus
—then blow a few kisses at Narcissus?

Aren't you just another little guy
trapped in Human Ken's frame?

Maybe I am smoke and mirrors; ectoplasm
and corsets, face-paint and hairpieces
rolled into a snake charmer,
but who's the snake and who's the charmer here?
Because snake charming is all optics—
not melody, but movement.
Like self-absorbed folks, snakes are bad
listeners as they have no ears; it's the visual
impact that mesmerizes,
the pungi player's thrust and sway register
as threat so the cobra undulates
keeping lidless eyes on the seeming menace.

I admire the pungi player—if you attend, you
hear no break in song, the player
uses circular breathing and laser-like
control to piece a seamless song; a yogic dancer
he fingers breath and cue—lithely
the snake follows—spellbound.

See you on the screen where
all is just as it appears,

Valeria

Redress

(RE) TURN IV

The unforeseen metaphor

It seems, then, that we're fairly well agreed that an imitator
has no worthwhile knowledge of the things he imitates,
that imitation is a kind of game and not something to be taken seriously,
and that all the [tragic] poets, whether they write in iambics
or hexameters, are as imitative as they could possibly be.
(Republic 601b, 602b)

Therefore, isn't it just that such poetry should return from exile
when it has defended itself in lyric or any other metre?
(Republic 607d)

I was wandering in Plato's Just city and don't know how I ended up in Plastic's Republic, but there I was, gazing up at the sun trying to get my bearings when a dapper stripling approached me and introduced himself as Ken.

Socrates, there you are, he said, showing no surprise, though we were dressed quite differently. I asked him how he knew my name; imagine my shock when he told me that I am a famous ancient philosopher and still revered by some as the wisest and most just of men. He had checked me out on Wikipedia.

He brought me to an ornate, roseate temple with a smooth, lustrous exterior. Welcome to the Dream House, there's Barbie, waiting at the door. Ken gently guided me to the tall, very thin woman wearing a short tunic the colour of cherry blossoms. Her blue, over-bright eyes and bubbly manner scared me a bit, but she warmly called me by name, took my arm and led me to a couch. As is my custom, I propped myself on cushions and was soon sipping rosé wine.

Please excuse all the pink, Socrates, she said. It isn't my colour of choice, but it's part of my character and some think it a useful fiction for girls to believe that pink is for females and blue for males. Appearance is crucial in this city and I have to model endless dress codes for young girls.

I asked her why I was brought to this strange place made of a material I could not identify.

It's plastic, Socrates—the stuff I'm made of—a magical substance that liquefies when heated and can imitate almost anything in nature; when it cools and hardens, it lasts forever.

That would make it eternal, Barbie, can it be the soul of this Republic?

She looked mystified but never lost her smile. People use this word and talk about soulful things, Socrates, but I don't know what they're on about. I strike all kinds of realistic poses that resemble a real woman, but the only life I have comes from girls who use me to play out their little dramas. As far as plastic goes, it's miraculous manmade stuff that can be fashioned to look like wood, flowers, stone—almost anything—even flesh. It's what I call the 3 M's: mouldable, mobile and modern—like me.

Suddenly, she ran from the room and another woman entered who was plumper, her hair an ungodly shade of blue and wearing a close-fitting tunic. What has happened to Barbie? I asked. I thought it rude of her to dash off like that and send a stranger in her place.

I am Barbie, Socrates.

And I could tell by her voice and manner, that she could be, but I remained bewildered.

I've been made over. For decades, I have been accused of corrupting young girls and been banished from many homes. My accusers say my physical perfection disrespects true women and I've become a false goddess for girls who worship my look and develop all manner of disorders—so here I am as "Curvy Barbie."

But it is wrong to *not* look like Barbie and *be* Barbie at the same time. That's playing games with reason, it deceives and confuses. *Not-Barbies* should not be made to perform as Barbies and be called by the same name.

Exactly what I told the designers at Mattel, Socrates. Still, with these four different bodies they've given me, I really am Barbie and not Barbie, you could say. Plastic is my essence and allows it; aside from having a malleable body, I am a go-with-the-flow being and can become any doll-persona the market demands. Can plasticity be my soul?

No, the soul is the opposite of changeable things and is immutable. You seem more durable than eternal.

That may be, but I embody a workable spirit and may reflect the modern soul of an unpredictable republic.

Modern soul? Another contradiction! You really are an actor, Barbie—an imitation in more ways than one. First you appear to be a miniature female, then as a performer you change your appearance to look like any number of different women. I imagine that you also speak as many personas uttering verses (perhaps denigrating mathematics) without regard to their moral effect and probably strike both comic and tragic poses. You are imitation upon imitation, imprisoning citizens in the world of appearance—like all poets I banished from the Just Republic.

You could say I represent the ultimate female imitation, but this is my lot, Socrates. Mattel created me and I bear the company stamp on my neck. I'm never referred to as a doll and all their stories and little vignettes pass me off as a living woman. But I'm more than a beauty, I'm also sold as a costumed role model so girls can playact the future. I've had over 100 careers and run for U.S. president 6 times. "Imagine the possibilities," they jingle to convince mothers that I am a beneficial friend.

Who is this Mattel? He sounds like a sophist spewing the worst rhetoric.

Maybe—is your sophist in marketing? The poet who stuck me in this Plastic's Republic calls your rhetoric, *spin*. She's written verses that force me to be her truth-seeking doll. Mattel is all about profit and if I want to exist, I have to keep the dollars rolling in so they devise new Barbies and new dramas to mask all that. To sell, I must perform as a most desirable and good companion.

Mattel *is* a Sophist then, but poets are no better. They're both the worst kind of imitators. Poets inflame the passions; their lyrics create images that are unreal, their word-music beguiles and leads the soul away from reason into imagination.

I'm all about imagination but speaking of your Republic, didn't you create a just city by using words and creating images?

Yes, I had to use words and images to build it, but my dialogues do not rile the emotions, instead, they use reason to seek virtue and uncover the just city. Even if it is a mythical place, some fictions are better than others.

I'm unreal Socrates, but not simply bad. I also wear costumes that make me a doctor, an athlete an architect or teacher, but all the judges talk about is my body. Maybe it depends which fiction girls choose to wear. In the end, I create a make-believe city and girls can only be citizens there for a limited time, then I am discarded and they move on except for a few Human Barbies who can't grow up.

Come to think of it, Barbie, you and I do have some things in common; I was executed for corrupting the youth of Athens and put to death.

I've been beheaded more than once and executed in all kinds of ways.

I see why that might happen to you, but let me follow my train of thought. You say your poet has kidnapped you from the playroom and put you into a book of poems to show citizens that they can stop dancing to Mattel's musical colourings and question the truth behind your charming face and façade. Plato dragged me from the grave into his dramatic dialogues, gave me a voice and still forces me to debate any topic he wants to examine with a myriad cast of wise-guys. Like you, I can hardly keep up. One day I'm arguing with Glaucon and Thrasymachus on Justice, another, I'm questioning Hippias on Beauty, then you can find me discussing Piety with Euthyphro and on and on.

I see the similarity, Socrates—and the difference—you must be as wise as I am popular, but aren't we both imaginary characters in our respective Republics? I think my poet would say that she and Plato are both lovers of goodness. They're both sounding off to break the hypnotic spell of spin doctors and have people redirect their eyes and look above and beyond—and both have only the power of artful words for truth-telling and truth seeking.

It's hard to know who's speaking when you go on like that. But here I am Plato's doll who banished poets from the Republic, dialoguing with you, Barbie, the poet's doll imitating a philosopher. By Zeus! We need more pink wine.

Discard

The uniqueness of an object is surrendered
when we agree to reproduction.
(Walter Benjamin)

Limbs akimbo, discarded she lay
in a curbside box, amid a dapper Ken
and opulent velvet-garbed Barbie
among a gaggle of no-name knockoffs.

High broad cheekbones
blue almond eyes, long ponytail,
she was tee-clad on top
nude on the bottom, looking
like a screwed Natasha lured West
for mean play then abandoned
on a mattress of soiled dreams.

Rummaging, I found the chic denim outfit,
a label to put things right—this
was no tossed-off tart, no
Barbie wannabe, but a real
Mary-Kate and Ashley doll, carnal
authenticity stamped on her neck.

How far she was now from that super
spa day video, how far
from the Olsen Twins brand spun
from childhood's gold,
a once-real face bought
and sold, smiling
to this cautionary end.

Barbie Sounds Out

1

babes play
babes say ba ba   Ba rrr b e
be a ba be   be be a   bo db y
be a bar   bar   Bar bie
i.e. bare ly   a bod y be
be   no ~~body~~

2

Barbie breasts bar   barbarian nipples
nipples be a no-no
ra-ra- ra   no bra   no brainer
know   no nipples   on breasts
now know   breasts bear no nipples,
know how busty Barbie be   no B-cup cupcake
Barbie bar-hops   big-breasted
in bed or bar nipple   less
nip nip nipples? yes! pin-up Barbie   no less

3

barring the   BRRR   of barbed air-waves
Barbie babble   in ear
her barbed scat   on air
air on a B string
airheads put on   airs
hair-heads rarely   hear
how barbarian girls reared on   hair play
buy Barbie babble
be nobody   no~~body~~

buy Barbie and   be
rabbi Barbie   or   A-rab Barbie
or Barbara-Ann bomb, bomb, bomb
bomb, bombing Iran

4

grab Barbie by the waist
no way
Barbie brags a barely-there   waist

waist-away   be done
waste-away   be none

Redecorating the Dream House

As this fashion mogul gins up excess
a pink front cues the dream's inner life;
wall stones cut as pony-tailed silhouettes,
scrollwork B's galore ape bouncy chic;
gilt high-heel doorknobs initiate entrants
through that signature hook.

Pink washes the swish Betsy Ross
cum Martha Stewart décor, pushes
3 floors & 7 bedrooms of rosy promise
feasting on forever apple-pie
steaming in the whimsy kitchen.

Elect dolls thrive in bubble-gum air,
the roseate few fit for monochrome living
settle into a strawberry-cream couch;

flamingo curtains are drawn at dusk
when blushing chandeliers mantle rooms
in sunset sheen s-mothering other pigments.

In this cotton-candy nation
mono-manic teeny boppers get hooked
on woman-evasion, follow a Lolita-look
rulebook dictated by a one-value rich kid.

But true stargazers yawn at Mattel's
sugar-choke and since visionaries mix
chance palettes, poet and protestor ask:
Where are America's child dreamers
and asylum seekers? Didn't Barbie's forebears
heed the Mother of Exiles' beacon?
Haven't all settlers obeyed stomach rumblings,

refused the explosive fists of war-hawks
and two-bit traders—the tinpot dictator's nightmare?

Each child hankers after a safe house for reverie
says the Barbie muse—let's pitch pink to the wind,
fling open gates and welcome kaleidoscopic lassies
and homeless hopefuls by making over
this sleepy puppet-pad.

And lickety-split wide-eyed whiz kids
re-member the entrance with real stargazers
like Sojourner Truth's sepia stare asking
ain't I a woman? They usher the trio of Kate Millet,
Simone de Beauvoir and Angela Davis
into the gilded frame, tell Stacey,
Chelsea and Skipper to push off.

And above the soft seating, mass-market florals
under-paint Harriet Tubman's efflorescent freedom train
and La Pasionaria's body blooming anti-fascist barricades,
all dream-driven kin to *Liberty Leading the People*.

Break out
the *Royal Albert Old Country Roses* china,
set the table for another Boston Tea Party.

Dream House Coda
The Barbie Library: Selected Titles

Bookshelves in the 2014 Dream dwelling
house pleather-bound volumes,
etched spines flourishing Victorian motifs
—unlettered hardbacks, title-less.

A minstrel poet then, sees fit to refute
the jingle, re-muse hack lyrics and sing:

"Summer days are breezy
our library's brain-pleasing (at the Dream House)
everyone's excited,
your thoughts can be ignited
by dipping into pages
of tomes writ by sages (at the Dream House)."

And to make sound sense,
to shelves, she adds:

A Barbie's Garden of Verses
A Room of Barbie's Own
Socialism or Barbieism
Bar-being and Nothingness
The Second Sex-Doll
The Princess
A Doll for All Seasons
Barbiemorphosis
The Barbiad
One Dimensional Dolls
The Barbie Mystique
Paradise Sold
Paradise Recycled

On Barbie Mutilation

A two-faced art object and thrift-store find,
as dolls go, Barbie ranks her own class,
poses the mother of all doll questions
—to buy or not to buy.

More than a mere add-on to the doll heap,
she musters a good-girl, bad-girl riddle,
as singular name and calculated megastar,
she arrives at juvenilia's reception
as debutante empress—an open-ended
guest-of-honour; a durable rite-of-passage
flogging risky futures, rolling out
a red carpet to who knows where.

Venerated over knock-offs,
over time, the Mattel-tagged totem
loses her beau ideal lustre, wanders
into state-of-nature territory where childhood's
soulful citizens become Marquis De Sade brats
questing for the inside story, desecrating
the tacit first principle,
I still own the mould.

Who Executes

Between Mattel ideal   and ideal purchaser
                    the child,
between the gift   and handover
                Barbie

cool plastic skin sutured to human hands

but to what end   her beginning   becoming

          who executes her ends?

As far back as the pre-Diversity era
little mavericks were disrupting
the dictatrix doll, updating grown-up,
back-of-the box directions. Before
Barbie Fascistas gave us *types* and *shades,*
self-empowering iconoclasts reworked her assets.

One self-espousing tomboy made over
that flinty figure by hack-sawing her
in-your-face breasts; the "boobectomy"
freed things up—Barbie could flat-out
let loose, own G.I. Joe's shirt.

Surrounded by frosty Barbies,
African-American girls puzzled whether
exclusive pulchritude aped the master race;
in a jiffy, magic-markers rallied *Black is beautiful*
to Ebony-over hoary error so whitewashed
(un) truths showed vitiligo streaks, springing
blackened Barbie to run on Washington.

A budding doctor craving oxford-wearing
gravitas, fixed dolly's feet to stove,
took down the enforced stiletto, close-cropped
the blast of hair, and in rousing
revision, detailed owlish horn-rims
schooling vacant baby-blues.

A yearning to bend Barbie to Ken
brought on brutal rupture: sidewalk thumps
levelled breast to chest,
wax (flesh-tinted) smartly plugged gaping
craters, girded up the hourglass waist.
Ankles gaily snapped, base pedestals
reformed, fit for sensible shoes.

Then snip, snip, snip curls
acetone scrub the lady-face to mug
an androgynous air; let Ken's baggy pants
temper too-shapely legs.
Where did Barbie go?

          And who's to say?
for a diverse two can cross either way,
a campy wig from Mattel's hair-play,
a wispy negligeé (pink, *s'il vous plait*)
and marbles superglued on pecs transport
Ken to her facsimile.

The icon's ruin runs amok from
ludic vice, boredom-sprung—
(boredom births all evil, says Kierkegaard).

Depraved brothers Oster-blend Barbie
or slam her head in a drawer, G I Joe
murders his girl, she's married off to a dinosaur.

Barbie gallows and hearse-led funerals,
twenty guillotined heads
unearthed beneath the forest floor.

When spanked bottoms burn, firecrackers blast
the queen to kingdom-come—limbs torn,
temper-tossed—plastic reduced to dust.*

---

* Talking bobble-heads at Mattel did not respond to requests for interviews about
these abuses.

Barbs Poetica

Isn't mutilation what poets do?
Aren't these Barbie-blasters surreal lyricists
realizing the bounty of the world
exists to be recast by rebarbative bards?

Haven't poets always bashed public figures,
rehashed doublespeak with unique figures of speech?
Isn't Barbie prime for violent versifiers to gag her singular
synecdoche and monotonous metonymy?
Partial to stock response, she's no heroic epic of the distaff.

Haven't poets always snapped the strings
of Madison Avenue lyres and, Dada-like,
slashed-and-scissored Wall Street's pinstripe blab,
ripped into Chanel's allegory machined
into fast fashion by wage slaves?

Isn't a poet a suicide bomber—language strapped
to chest, heart pulsing ticking letters?
Isn't the Muse forever wiring? Fusing scribbler to pen,
to detonate as verse, irradiate as dazzling ruckus?

Aren't poetics detectives of likeness in
difference, questing for a fresh score in simile,
shadowing the unforeseen metaphor?

And aren't poets contrary path builders
diverting to the road not taken
drafting freeways to the othered side?
Isn't progress … transgression?

Doesn't vision bend diction—bum-steer the poem
to intersect and show itself—transcribing feminine
rhyme to a masculine line, cross-dressing
old-hat couplets, cutting loose in free verse?

Aren't poets beret-wearing Beats (or renegade priests)
springing incarcerated rhythms,
rerouting lines, migrating via enjambment
or camping via juxtaposition?

Isn't every lyricist an underground guerrilla,
a black asterisk starring the blanched page?
Isn't ink against erasure?

Barbie Rejoinder: Mirror

If well used, the mirror can aid
moral meditation between woman and herself
(Socrates Barbie)

My blonde merit, breasts and booty
are such stuff as vision is made on—
not *my* fault I'm flawless.

See me true   a tempered looking glass,
your desire reaching for inter face.

Despite the mute, senseless fun
axiom-perfect killjoys make of me,
I'm not a heartless beauty-dealer
or one-dimensional glamour queen,

not the yellow-brick road or play-binding trance;

I'm the make-believe face of a woman possessed
a *toy* lady-in-waiting, the consummate handmaid
manhandled by blood-curdling girls.

Only low-blow poets or backroom philosophers
size me up as virtuoso siren, stupefy
to hoodwinked gamer, flesh-and-brain daughters.

I'm no *who's-who* blurring body-lines,
to peddle myself into you—*au contraire,*

any young miss can squelch my moniker,
rechristen and customize Mattel's bunco spin,
some reclaim me as dormant fairy-tale
others maim in cut-throat horror games.

An unfinished act, I'm a puppet resounding
femme-fatale or feminist panache;
I affect alchemy that suits, dialogue as *you* will,
echo, reflect Snow White's human look;

any girl, any woman before any mirror
begging the question (?answer)

to which I am the answer (?question)

I-doll Supreme

Although I still punch above my weight
even the plus-sized, blue-maned Fashionista (me?)
at sixty, maybe I've lived past my Self

outlived Barbara Millicent Roberts,
hazing a faint remember-when. Today
I'm on first-name basis with the world

like Cher, Madonna, Beyoncé or God

my Midwest beginnings eclipsed by brand-rule
I'm a clipped two-syllable Barbie, no past on view.

Long-gone the *Always Barbie* of bygone days
days of blonding-the-course in sun-licked supremacy
one body reigning in resolute dimension

(girls see Barbie as flaxen and fair
the bon-bon brunette and titian-haired ginger
only pretenders summing to second fiddle).

I've slighted time's human face, blessed
cutting-edge tweaks; decades of trifling
change shaped by my aura of dominant

restraint—eleven deliberate inches
the guarded silhouette yielding
three generations of Wall Street devotees,

a classic who captured 150 countries,
dressed by Dior, Armani, Chanel, et al
hard-nosed designers lured by an haute-doll.

My spell held, fast and holy until
the crash into day-traders' hell when
I fell to a stock market tragedy

resurrected as Mattel's avenging angel
of *real-world diversity*. I don't admit lineage
in that "Lovin' Leopard Curvy, Cheerful Check Petite,

Blue Beauty Tall" Barbie mash-up,
to shrink or grow or put on weight,
to flat-foot the arch is so NOT-Barbie

just the toss of a sleight-of-hand pragmatist
jingoing a *keep-your-eye-on-the-Barbie*, shell game
(if you're not appearing you're disappearing).

Last round — twenty-eight mutations and counting
it's not the tally but ongoing hustle, my neck a pivot
doing a double take on each translation

only to spot myself as Pity Dolly or millennial
Barbie Warbucks raising an army to rout
the Elsa craze, crush Disney's turncoat princess.

My finest coup was fixing American retail
in God's playground, doubling as
the One's untimely soul.

DOLLS IN THE DARK

I won't endure these half-filled
human masks; better the puppet. It at least is full.
I'll put up with the stuffed skin, the wire, the face
that is nothing but appearance.

(Rilke)

TURN V

I can bond with inanimate things

And if someone compelled him to look at the light itself, wouldn't his eyes hurt, and wouldn't he turn around and flee towards the things he's able to see, believing that they're really clearer than the ones he's been shown.

(Republic, 518b)

Though few souls are tall enough to face the sun, he glossed each flesh and blood goddess walking towards him as Beauty; some seekers confuse the dazzle of self-reflection with the arrival of the philosopher moment.

Though Woman is now a grounded moon, back then, he elevated all lovelies brushing up against his heart to the highest good, believed, despite his lack of physical capital, that he was due his own beauty. The reverie fluttered and took wing as a larger-than-life Eros in his corner, firing dove feathers on his behalf. Willfully, he turned a blind eye to the double-sexed hellion, the leaden owl feathers in his quiver. "Why not me?" he mused. Silvering his tongue with odes on Truth beyond corporeal limits, he eclipsed the guttural naysayers in his head.

But the shadowy world of courtship is ruled by sublunary females whose vision is as capricious as flesh. No serenade or witty rhyme could efface his homely sin inflamed by puberty's flare-ups and scarred, pitted skin. Try as he might, love remained a no-go horizon, a moving-target. The pile up of women turning sharply away, side-lined him to a shame-faced nobody. When he mustered the nerve to tender a night out, feminist evasion and ladylike aversion wounded more than a direct *not interested*. One night, the I'm-not-feeling-well Aphrodite showed up at the local pub, an arm-piece for a natty soldier; the goddess of love twisted into a heartless harlot and no sign of Eros on the barstool beside him.

Too many solo sunrises stung his eyes, driving him to turn away from the harsh glare. Safely indoors, he lowered the blinds; the dim light softened the arc of too much sky around him. This refuge, made cozy by enduring objects, calmed him: the well-loved poster fixed to the wall, the upright spines of books, his guitar hanging from a nail—all rock-solid companions—anchors to himself. An earthy affection for these life-sustaining pals became palpable; there was the old Chevy too, another long-time buddy who made him top dog of the road. This side-trip ended in an epiphany, the realization that human relationships are skin-deep and too temporal, a flaw pointing to a deep truth.

The enduring bond with things, their promise of a humane fidelity summoned a bygone reverie. Out of his reflection, shades served up gingerbread cookies and the boyish shadow-play of Arthur and Merlin. Dressed in robes, two-handing his broadsword, he powered up the medieval force and turned beautiful; he would alchemize the laws of nature, reject the ritual dance and source his own Camelot. Why risk stepping beyond 1 (the loneliest number), relating as 2— holding Two transcendent in One?

But he pined for a quiescent body, fuelled his yen by playing drums and singing along to soulful hurtin' songs in a passionate falsetto. If only the bloody horizon would release him—for those Jezebels will never stop running off with chichi guys and sit still like the silicone girls he'd seen online who could see past his face into his soul. If only he could break the female bind, unchain his heart and steady this bent—keep his eyes fixed on a sure-thing.

Soon he'll move into a Playboy magazine, divine his love and emerge as a plastic playmate's boyfriend. Each morning he'll dress and pose his yielding poster-girl, hold her close each night until she warms to flesh.

Pygmalion: Keep Your Walls in Place

And carved in ivory such a maid, so fair,
As nature could not with his art compare ...
    (Ovid)

Amathus, Cyprus where cocky daughters of Propoetus
dare deny Venus—goddess of love, of irked grace;
divine fury torpedoes their home,
mints the first hookers: pride turfs
them to the street to openly hock flesh.

Cursed blood congeals, stain fades
in bloodless cheeks, bodies mineralize
to petrified women.

Such depraved femmes chill Pygmalion,
give cause to freeze the city in female flaw.
Aren't all women stone-cold whores?
Better cut to the studio, turn his shivering heart
to sculpting a utopia chastened
by hand-buffed good-girls.

But a frosty bed flusters wakened fingers
kindles his tool so marble warms, purrs
and intimates a too-true breast nearing breath,
a maid assuming a come-hither look,
if only virtue could be outdone.

He dotes on virgin stone, stokes
it to almost-urging flesh;
the *inamorato* strokes his handiwork
until she yields to kisses that feel
returned enough to kiss again.
Fondling creamy thighs, so lost in love is he
he checks for bruises.

And playing a closet swain sparks fervent fun:
roses, silk, emeralds quicken life's flame
in love's facsimile who looks exquisite dressed
but no less nude, dreaming against
flowering linens—a sublime bedfellow.

Pygmalion kinks in house—no need to blush;
to keep walls in place, he sweet talks Venus
venerates Love to breed beyond art—
and charmed by bootlick prayer, the goddess
grants the deviant-boon, blesses union
of artist and ideal—to them
bestows a son, Paphos called,
founder of an eponymous walled city
nowhere near Lesbos.

Larry

Welcome to RealDoll, the world's finest love doll! Click on the individual thumbnails to see how RealDoll faces look with different bodies, skin tones and features. Real Dolls feature our patented Face-X-System which allows you to have multiple interchangeable faces with one body.

(Abyss Creations)

I can't get a girlfriend
because of my looks, my face
is like ten miles of bad road.
Acne scarred my skin but women
scored my heart. And with two
military bases nearby—stacks
of flashy young men around
to power up the dark.

It might seem radical, but I'd come
to a dead end with women, the ones I met
are all snake oil: games, distance, the cold shoulder,
all the times I've been used, the lies and flimflam,
never again. They don't intimidate me now—
nothing I want from them.

Here's a picture of the only woman
I've ever been with—Pamela, so wrapped
in chaos, the air around us, jumped
moved out late fall, '98,
I spent her Christmas money on myself
best thing she ever did for me was go.

That left me thinking how relationships
with humans are only temporary
left me wanting more. Here's a different picture,
me with Ginger and Kelly on either side.

Before I got Ginger Brooke and Kelly Sue
I was open country, everyone's doormat
Now, it's all about me and that is how it will stay.
And as good as the sex is, peace of mind's even better:

3 guns, 2 girls, 1 broad sword and my drums
like being your own god in your own world.

I can bond with inanimate objects
maybe I'll have them buried with me
I'm a small guy, we'd fit in an oversized coffin
we can all turn to dust together.

Larry and Ginger Brooke

She's like a blow-up, but solid silicone
pliable, flexible with a stainless-steel skeleton,
heavy too—people-heavy. Being loose jointed
she can't stand but rests sitting
or lying down, like the website says—
the poise and grace of a sleeping woman.

They only had three body types back then,
I chose style one. Three was tall and voluptuous
too much weight—besides, I like natural looking
women. Looking for a face, Brooke Shields
struck me, shining grey eyes, lush hair
a come-hither star I could make a wish on;
damn, I told myself she's sweet enough to eat,
so, it came to me how, as a kid
I loved gingerbread.

Took me ten months to save the money;
I ordered Ginger Brooke in January
she arrived late spring—remember it
just like yesterday—too wired to eat,
a sleepless night of waking dreams.
Up 4 hours before the usual time, waiting
for light to wash up a new dawn—I tore
to the window every time a truck roared by.

She arrived seated in a Styrofoam-lined wooden crate
double-strapped around the neck and waist,
a single silk carnation between her feet.

In her black satin slip, against a pure white background
my fresh angel of mercy faced me,

I moved her to the couch using the suggested bridal lift.

Why Two

Getting Ginger Brooke was like winning
a billion dollars or speeding in my dream car.
The feeling of racing my wheels on a time line
going nowhere dropped away, I had already backed off
now I turned in; every day after work, the weather-beaten
door unlatched my girl—unwavering fulfillment
waiting on the couch or bed where I had set her.

I like dressing Ginger, but no thongs or stilettos
nothing tarty, just a cotton, lace-trimmed nightie
or snow-white blouse and grey pleated skirt
the colour of rain. After our first summer,
the monkey was off my back.

Why two?

Right after my order, body type four arrived—
petite, light, only four eleven, ninety pounds.
That got me hankering for a blonde and I wondered
if they really are more fun, maybe it was only greed—
how having is only a lead-up to craving.

Funding my curiosity was a problem
until I realized a personal loan
would up my credit rating. At the bank
the scrubbed-straight credit officer
asked what the money was for.
I whipped out a picture of Ginger
"To buy another doll like this,"
then scanned her face as she puzzled it out
"Oh, you use them for photography,"

Sizing up such wholesome guesswork
the sideswipe rose in me, "Sometimes,
but mostly we just have sex." Her face crashed
she pitched up, itching to run—muttered
that she'd phone about the approval.

Slipping out of her office,
I took the butterscotch leather chair
"I'll just wait here until you let me know."
In a jiffy she breezed in, yelling
"You're good to go"—I'll say—they whisked
my lewd little ass out of there.

Kelly Sue's Sonnet

How do I love you? This real doll you own
Loves you with Galatea's pristine fingers,
The curve of famished lips, heat that lingers
On this too-cool angel shell; with keepsake moans
Of roses spiralling through projected ears.
I love being your wounded traveller's balm,
Posed each morn—a hard-won 23rd psalm,
A wind-up bride arresting gone-girl fears.

Women's leggy ways and straying sweets I do
Not wish on you—my dresser, mother, lover.
In idle air, I sing no on-ice blues,
Belie no beating heart, seek no favours
From romantic poets or rapper men;
I'm good wife—yours—my tongue and pen.

AFTERLIFE
(WORD)

North Pacific Garbage Gyre

I

Hot equatorial winds spiral, commix, currents whirl
whip round the North Pacific Gyre once an ocean dervish
now a concentric garbage swirl

One-hundred million tons, offhand vortex of squashed cups,
crushed bottles, bobbing Ziploc bags, fused six-pack rings,
twisting dolls, balls, Bics, yesterday's plastic bits

rush downstream, gush non-stop into weeks months years
the collective unconscious glut, caught in river's junked maw
disgorged into pollution's Sargasso.

Left to our own ends, refuse all ends where life began
in once-sane waters—on our aqua sea face we pitch
unknown, unseen, afar, a new rubbish continent.

II

High noon on too-calm waters
a manmade mantle bars the sun
the autotroph's future darkens, I know
but don't show me

what Charles Moore sighted—
no more pristine ocean, but a Pacific
vomiting endless plastic—no
don't show me

reckless freight carriers struck
by the storm's *o'ertaking wings*
the candy-coloured crate's sway and topple,

quieten the jetsam

running off with my peace of mind, a tsunami
of unliquidated Nike sneakers, rubber ducks
hockey gloves, socking the brain
don't show me

sea foam hurling up the aquatic dead
crazy miles of branded bags—salt-thinned
strands that mock jellyfish and poison sea turtles
silence the ocean's

flotsam roar curling into a death-mute
conch sinking, abysmal, beneath
the whole caboodle—no lifeline;
tomorrow I'll come around

wake from sleep's ringed underbelly strangling
seabirds and in the wake of sail boats strung
on the horizon, I'll find myself—missing, at sea
downhill from everything.

III

Work quick—too slow—tight-fisted
incessant hustle; disposable suns
flicker as the world's poor pull chariots
of cheap goods across the sky.

The World Packaging Organization
takes the *on-the go lifestyle's* compulsive pulse,
graphs the *time-poor consumer's* steadfast
unconcern for environmental-cide.

Morning breaks on blister-packed muffins
afternoon pops clamshell containers
housing huge, flavour-looted berries,
triple-wrapped evenings muffle trash bins.
Growth scents the air with doublespeak:

recycle, rebuy, regurgitate, remember
there's opportunity in the breakdown
of the sit-down family dinner
and while families break down—plastic
is forever.

Acknowledgements

Thanks to Michael Mirolla and Connie McParland for approving publication of *Plastic's Republic* to coincide with Barbie's 60th birthday; their generosity and patience granted much needed space for study and musing. To Diane Bracuk for years of energetic and tenacious boosting of my poetics and of Barbie as epic subject, for her keen editorial eye and savvy guidance in all aspects of this project. To Nada Conic, Greek, Latin and Plato scholar and long-time friend for her intelligence and artistry in editing the poems and for her empathic, ambitious and artful direction as we pondered Barbie, plastic, and Plato. Her customary brilliance, attuned heart and ear wedded to a devoted grammarian, grace this collection. To my beloved partner, George Elliott Clarke, for winging us to an idyllic summer apartment in Tropea, Calabria, where some of these poems were written. Aside from adroit perusal of individual poems over the years, his editorial insights and mighty wordsmithing helped fine-tune the finished work. To Doreen Bracuk for the inspirational treasure trove of sumptuously clad dolls and full wardrobe of Barbie couture designed and sewn by her, decades ago; and to Franceszka Kolatacz for timely support and the authentic and ravishing Fulla doll. To Rafael Chimicatti who expertly and mindfully worked with me on the cover design. Thanks finally, to Mattel for numerous tone-deaf nuggets that astounded the odd poetry editor and to authors, journalists and You-Tube enthusiasts who helped make Barbie my strange bedfellow.

Thanks to the editors of the following anthologies and journals where some of these poems appeared: *Exploring Voice: Italian Canadian Female Writers* (*Italian Canadiana*, Vol. 30), *Soglie* (University of Pisa, Italy), *Maple Tree Literary Supplement*, *A Filo Doppio* (Donzelli Editore, Italy), *Voices in Italian-Americana* (USA), *Dis(s) sent, Ocean State Review* (USA), *Potent Potables* (upcoming).

About the Author

Giovanna Riccio is a graduate of the University of Toronto where she majored in philosophy. Her poems have appeared in national and international journals and magazines as well as numerous anthologies. Translations of her poems have been published in Italian, French, Spanish, and Romanian. She is the author of *Vittorio* (Lyricalmyrical Press, 2010) and *Strong Bread* (Quattro Books, 2011) which was shortlisted for The Relit Award. Giovanna has lectured and performed at national and international events including Blue Met, The Edinburgh Fringe, Seamus Heaney Homeplace and The Association of Italian-American Studies Conference at the University of Calabria, Italy.

MIX
Paper from
responsible sources
FSC® C100212

Printed in January 2019
by Gauvin Press,
Gatineau, Québec